KING ARTHUR

EXCALIBUR UNSHEATHED

AN ENGLISH LEGEND

STORY BY
JEFF LIMKE

PENCILS AND INKS BY
THOMAS YEATES

ADAPTED FROM
SIR THOMAS MALORY'S
LE MORTE D'ARTHUR

SCOTLAND

Hadrian's Wall

IRISH SEA

IRELAND

WALES

CORNWALL

KING ARTHUR

EXCALIBUR UNSHEATHED

AN ENGLISH LEGEND

NORTH SEA

London

Thames River

ENGLAND

FLANDERS

NORMANDY

GRAPHIC UNIVERSE™ MINNEAPOLIS

WHETHER KING ARTHUR WAS A REAL PERSON IS UNKNOWN, BUT HIS STORY IS SET AMID REAL EVENTS IN BRITISH HISTORY. HE WOULD HAVE LIVED AROUND A.D. 400 OR 500, WHEN THE MANY SMALL KINGDOMS OF ENGLAND, WALES, AND CORNWALL WERE FIGHTING EACH OTHER AND AGAINST FOREIGN INVADERS. ARTHUR IS THUS SEEN AS THE KING WHO UNITED AND DEFENDED EARLY BRITAIN. BUT OFTEN ARTHURIAN TALES ARE DEPICTED AS TAKING PLACE MUCH LATER IN THE MIDDLE AGES (ABOUT 1100–1300), WITH KNIGHTS IN ARMOR, JOUSTS, AND CASTLES. EXCALIBUR UNSHEATHED FOLLOWS THAT TRADITION.

STORY BY JEFF LIMKE

PENCILS AND INKS BY THOMAS YEATES
SPECIAL THANKS TO TOD SMITH

COLORING BY HI-FI DESIGN

LETTERING BY BILL HAUSER

Graphic Universe
An imprint of Lerner Publishing Group
241 First Avenue North
Minneapolis, MN 55401 U.S.A.

Website address: www.lernerbooks.com

Library of Congress Cataloging-in-Publication Data

Limke, Jeff.
    King Arthur : Excalibur unsheathed / by Jeff
Limke, adapted from Sir Thomas Malory's
Le Morte d'Arthur ; illustrations by Thomas
Yeates.
        p.   cm. — (Graphic myths and legends)
Includes index.
    ISBN-13: 978-0-8225-3083-1 (lib. bdg. : alk. paper)
    ISBN-10: 0-8225-3083-X (lib. bdg. : alk. paper)
    1. Graphic novels. I. Malory, Thomas, Sir, 15th
cent. Morte d'Arthur. II. Title. III. Series.
PN6727.L53S76 2007
741.5'973—dc22   2005010186

Manufactured in the United States of America
1 2 3 4 5 6 - JR - 12 10 09 08 07

TABLE OF CONTENTS

A COUNTRY WITHOUT A KING

LONG AGO, *UTHER PENDRAGON*, THE KING OF ENGLAND, DIED WITHOUT AN HEIR. RIVAL FACTIONS BATTLED AGAIN AND AGAIN FOR THE CHANCE TO BE CROWNED THE NEXT RULER.

MERLIN, WHO WAS OFTEN CALLED A MAGICIAN, SAW NO END TO THE CHAOS. HE KNEW *A KING HAD TO BE FOUND* BEFORE THE FIGHTING BETWEEN LORDS GOT OUT OF CONTROL. MERLIN URGED THE ARCHBISHOP OF CANTERBURY TO HOLD A SERIES OF *JOUSTING TOURNAMENTS* IN LONDON.

UPON UTHER'S DEATH, A *SWORD EMBEDDED IN A STONE* HAD MIRACULOUSLY APPEARED AT *WESTMINSTER ABBEY* NEAR LONDON. THE ARCHBISHOP AND MERLIN AGREED THAT EACH TOURNAMENT WINNER WOULD GET THE CHANCE TO SHOW HE WAS FIT TO BE KING BY PULLING THE SWORD FROM THE STONE.

LORDS FROM ALL OVER ENGLAND TREKKED TO *LONDON*, ALL WITH THE SAME INTENT—

—HOPING TO WIN THE CHANCE TO PULL THE SWORD EMBEDDED IN STONE AND IN DOING SO, BE NAMED KING OF ALL ENGLAND.

THE SUN IS ALMOST CLEAR OF THE HORIZON.

I SHOULD PERHAPS GET A NEW SQUIRE, *ARTHUR?*

HURRY, MY BOY, THE LONGER WE TWIDDLE ABOUT, THE LESS LIKELY WE'LL GET THERE IN TIME, ESPECIALLY IF YOU WANT TO SEE IT FIRST.

I'M WORKING, I'M WORKING.

KNOW ANYONE ELSE WILLING TO *LISTEN* TO YOU, KAY?

I AGREE WITH ARTHUR. HE'S THE BEST YOU'RE GOING TO FIND.

NOW, HOWEVER, WE MUST BE ON OUR WAY TO YOUR FIRST TOURNAMENT, KAY.

TIME TO SEE WHAT THE *FUTURE* HOLDS, EH?

WE MUST PUT IT *BACK*! THEY WILL ALL THINK WE ARE CHEATS!

OR THIEVES!

OOOf!

LET *ME* TRY!

Shk-shk-shksss

YOU THERE! WHAT ARE YOU DOING?!

HE HAD THE *SWORD*! THAT *BOY* PULLED THE SWORD!

HOLD. LET US NOT LEAP TO RASH ACTIONS.

I THINK, *ARCHBISHOP*, WE NEED SOME TIME TO MUSE UPON WHAT HAS HAPPENED HERE.

PERHAPS WE SHOULD HAVE THE WINNERS COME BACK LATER WHEN IT CAN BE DEMONSTRATED TO *ALL* WHO SHOULD BE KING.

A WISE THOUGHT, MERLIN. ONLY IN FRONT OF A GROUP OF KINGS AND KNIGHTS OF STATURE CAN WE HOPE FOR ANY AGREEMENT ON THIS MATTER.

AT THE NEW YEAR, WE SHALL SEE WHO WILL BE ABLE TO EXTRACT THE *BLESSED SWORD* FROM THE STONE.

AT THAT TIME HERE AT WESTMINSTER WILL STAND ALL WINNERS—

—AND THIS BOY!

THE NEW KING IN A NEW YEAR

When New Year's Day arrived, all the knights who had won their regional tournaments returned to take their turn at pulling the sword from the stone.

WHOSO PULLETH
OUT THIS SWORD

Each truly believed he would be the one to succeed and prove that he was to be the **NEXT TRUE KING** of England.

Arthur watched as each failed in his own spectacular fashion. Arthur **DREADED THE MOMENT** when he would step forward for his turn.

He had never held a true sword before he had pulled this very one. He had not even fought much, other than throwing mud clots at Kay after rainstorms, which usually ended with him and Kay wrestling ...

...and with Kay winning.

WHOSO PULLETH
OUT THIS SWORD

What was he going to do?

His hands felt clammy. His heart beat so fast he was afraid it would explode. His stomach did flip-flops as he watched.

What if he **COULDN'T** pull it again?

Or what would he do if...

HE DID IT!

LATER, ALL THE IMPORTANT LORDS FROM THROUGHOUT ENGLAND MET TO DECIDE THE FUTURE OF THE COUNTRY. THEY WERE NOT ALL READY TO CALL ARTHUR KING JUST BECAUSE HE HAD PULLED THE SWORD FROM THE STONE.

I WILL *NEVER* FOLLOW A BEARDLESS BOY!

HE PULLED THE SWORD, *KING LOT.* HE IS TO BE OUR KING AND EVEN YOURS IN FARAWAY ORKNEY.

HE DOESN'T EVEN *LOOK* LIKE A KING. I DOUBT HE WOULD MAKE A GOOD STABLE BOY!

HE'S UTHER PENDRAGON'S SON.

UTHER GAVE HIM TO ME, TRUSTING ME TO FIND THOSE WHO WOULD RAISE HIM WISELY AND SAFELY.

UTHER DIDN'T WANT HIS PRINCE AND HEIR TO BE MURDERED BY SOMEONE WHO WANTED TO BE THE NEXT KING.

HE DOES TRULY BEAR THE SEMBLANCE OF UTHER.

I PLEDGE TO ARTHUR.

LIES! I WILL *NEVER* FOLLOW HIM!

RATHER, I WILL DEFEAT HIM *MYSELF!*

MY LIEGE.

FATHER, PLEASE, *NO.* I'M *NOT* THE KING.

I'M JUST YOUR SON.

NO, ARTHUR, WHAT MERLIN SPEAKS IS *TRUE*. HE GAVE ME YOU AS AN INFANT TO RAISE AS MY OWN, WHICH I HAVE DONE.

BUT *I DON'T UNDERSTAND*.

I KNOW, BUT WE DO. IT IS TIME FOR YOU TO LEAVE MY CARE. I ASK ONLY ONE *BOON* OF YOU.

ANYTHING, FATHER.

ECTOR, ARTHUR, NOT FATHER.

BUT I BEG OF YOU TO *TAKE CARE OF KAY*. HE HAS LOVED YOU AS A BROTHER, AND I BELIEVE YOU HAVE LOVED HIM AS ONE AS WELL.

I *DO* AND ALWAYS *WILL*.

HAIL, ARTHUR, KING OF ENGLAND!

EVEN THOUGH HE HAD BEEN NAMED KING, THE CROWN WAS NOT YET UPON ARTHUR'S HEAD.

I DON'T THINK I CAN *DO* THIS.

I DON'T KNOW *ANYTHING* ABOUT BEING A KING.

I DON'T KNOW OF ANY KING WHO DID WHEN HE STARTED. IN FACT, ALL OF THE KINGS I EVER KNEW WERE *VERY SCARED* TO BECOME KING ONCE THEY THOUGHT ABOUT IT.

AND THEY WERE MUCH OLDER THAN YOU. THERE IS NO REASON TO THINK THAT YOU SHOULDN'T BE A BIT SCARED AS WELL.

BUT KING LOT SAID HE WOULDN'T FOLLOW ME. AND THERE WILL BE OTHERS. *I'M JUST A BOY.*

HOW DO I MAKE ADULTS LISTEN TO ME OR EVEN FOLLOW ME, EVEN IF I'M KING?

THIS IS JUST *TOO MUCH.*

YOU HAVE GOOD MEN WITH YOU. THE FACT THAT *THEY* BELIEVE IN YOU WILL INFLUENCE OTHERS AS MUCH AS YOUR VOICE.

LISTEN CAREFULLY TO THEM AND TO THEIR ADVICE, BUT LISTEN TO YOUR *HEAD* AND *HEART* AS WELL.

REMEMBER, YOU ARE ALWAYS *FREE TO CHOOSE* AS YOU WILL. THAT IS A KING'S RIGHT—

—BUT YOU ARE NOT FREE OF THE *CONSEQUENCES* THAT WILL ACCOMPANY YOUR CHOICES.

NOW, LET US FOCUS ON THE FIRST WORRY AT HAND: YOUR *CORONATION.*

TIME WOULD PASS AND ARTHUR WOULD LEARN MUCH, LISTENING TO NOT ONLY ECTOR BUT ALSO **BORS**, KING OF THE GAULS ...

–OF THIS KING CLAUDUS WILL NEED TO BE ADDRESSED.

... **BAN**, BORS'S BROTHER AND THE KING OF BENWICK ...

VERY GOOD! **VERY** GOOD! YOU'RE GETTING MUCH BETTER!

... **SIR BAUDWIN** ...

–TO **PROTECT** THIS LAND IN MY ABSENCE–

... **SIR KAY**

–CAN **NOT** RUN THE LAND.

YOU HAVE ALWAYS DONE WELL WITH ECTOR'S LAND. YOU WILL BE A GOOD SENESCHAL.

BUT...

NO "**BUTS**," BROTHER. I **TRUST** YOU.

... AND **LEODEGRANCE**, KING OF CAMELIARD.

THE OUTLYING KINGS ARE GATHERING...

MY KING, DID YOU **HEAR** ME?

THE LESSON TAUGHT TO KING LOT

As Merlin collected what he needed...

... ARTHUR AND HIS KNIGHTS PREPARED FOR BATTLE.

AT HIS SIDE SAT SIR BRASTIAS, SIR KAY, SIR ECTOR, SIR BAUDWIN, SIR BEDIVERE, AND OTHERS READY TO FIGHT FOR THEIR KING ...

... AND FOR THEIR KNIGHTLY HONOR.

BEFORE YOU LEAVE THE CASTLE WALLS, ALLOW ME TO RELEASE *THIS DUST* TO THE WINDS.

IT WILL MAKE YOUR ENEMIES BELIEVE FIVEFOLD OF YOUR KNIGHTS HAVE COME TO FIGHT THEM.

FIVEFOLD?

THAT MANY ARMORED AND TRAINED KNIGHTS AGAINST LOT'S PEASANT-TRAINED FORCES?

I WOULD THINK *THAT* WILL WORRY OLD KING LOT.

LOT, YOU CANNOT WIN.

BOY, YOU DO NOT *KNOW* WHAT I CAN DO.

YOU HAVE LOST, AND I WILL TAKE *EVERYTHING* FROM YOU BECAUSE I AM YOUR BETTER.

YOU SHALL TAKE...

...NOTHING!

THE COLLECTOR OF BEARDS

BUT HE WOULD FIGHT MANY MORE.

DEFENDING HIS FRIENDS...

...AND AVENGING OLD SCORES.

WE SHALL *DEFEAT* THIS CLAUDUS TOGETHER, BAN AND BORS.

MORE WOULD JOIN HIM, IN TIME SWELLING THE NUMBERS OF HIS KNIGHTS TO MORE THAN ONE HUNDRED.

I, *LUCAN*, SON OF LORD CORNEUS, VOW TO *PROTECT* AND *UPHOLD* THE WORD OF YOU, MY KING, KING ARTHUR.

AS DO I, *ULFIUS*, VOW TO DO THE SAME AND REMAIN AT YOUR SIDE UNTIL *DEATH* CLAIMS ME.

BUT THE FIGHTING WAS NOT ALWAYS SUCCESSFUL, NOR *WITHOUT A PRICE.*

EVERY BATTLE CALMED ONE AREA, BUT ANOTHER WOULD FILL WITH *CHAOS*...

... AND EACH TIME, ARTHUR WOULD RIDE FORTH.

HER FATHER IS YOUR ALLY, KING LEODEGRANCE.

RYONS, KING OF THE NORGALES, HOLDS HIM PRISONER NEAR CASTLE BEDEGRAINE.

LEODEGRANCE IS MY FRIEND, AND EVEN FOR NOTHING MORE THAN THAT I WOULD FIGHT FOR HIM—

—BUT TO SEE *HER* SAFE, I WOULD FIGHT A HUNDRED MORE TIMES.

NO CHILD SHOULD EVER FEAR FOR HER FATHER.

28

THE FOREST OF PELLINORE'S PAVILION WAS CLOSER THAN ARTHUR SUSPECTED.

—WILL DEFEAT YOU.

HOW *CAN* HE? I AM A KING WHO HAS WON MANY BATTLES. I HAVE NOT YET BEEN DEFEATED.

WHO ELSE WOULD DEFEAT HIM? WHO ELSE *COULD*?

YES, WHO...?

I AM WHO.

WHY, THANK YOU, FRIEND SPARROW.

MY BIRD FRIEND SAYS THIS IS WHERE HE ABIDES.

A GIFT FROM THE LADY OF THE LAKE

PELLINORE SHALL HAVE TWO SONS. THEY WILL NOT BE SURPASSED FOR BRAVERY BY ANY OTHER IN HIS KINGDOM AND BY VERY FEW IN YOURS.

THEY SHALL LIVE LIFE PURELY AND BECOME KNIGHTS WHO WILL SERVE YOU WELL.

YOU WILL KNOW THEM AS PERCIVALE AND LAMERAKE OF WALES.

BUT WHY WOULD THEY *SERVE* ME? HE DEFEATED ME. THEY SHOULD *CHALLENGE* ME INSTEAD.

YOU HAVE SHOWN THEIR FATHER MERCY. THEY WILL KNOW IT IS AN HONOR TO SERVE YOU.

BUT AS FOR THIS... IT IS BROKEN AND USELESS.

MY SWORD!

WHAT *NEED* OF IT HAVE YOU—

—WHEN *THAT* IS THE SWORD YOU WERE *BORN* TO WIELD?

IN TIME, THIS BOY KING WOULD BECOME A MAN, ARTHUR, KING OF ENGLAND AND WIELDER OF EXCALIBUR.

MORE ADVENTURES LIE IN HIS FUTURE, STORIES OF HIS LOVE AND BETRAYAL, LIFE AND DEATH, TRIALS AND TRIBULATIONS, BATTLES AND SUCCESSES, BEFORE HIS FINAL TALE IN WHICH HE WOULD LEAVE THIS WORLD FOR THE *ISLE OF AVALON*—

—WHERE HE REMAINS TO THIS DAY *WAITING TO RETURN* WHEN HE IS MOST NEEDED TO RESTORE ENGLAND TO THE GRANDEUR HE BUILT.

GLOSSARY

BOON: a favor given in answer to a request

CORONATION: a ceremony in which a ruler is crowned and takes possession of a kingdom. In England, traditionally, a king or queen is blessed by an archbishop, receives the royal robes, and has the crown placed on his or her head.

FACTION: a group within a larger group that fights against those in power. Factions may also fight against each other to gain power.

JOUST: a battle on horseback between two knights or among a group of knights. Jousts were often mock battles fought in tournaments. The purpose was to knock an opponent out of the saddle with a lance.

KNIGHT: a mounted soldier sworn to loyally serve a lord or ruler

LANCE: in jousting, a long, tapered spear carried by knights. In tournament jousts, lances had blunt tips and were made of dry wood. They broke easily without wounding or injuring contestants.

LIEGE: a superior, such as a lord or king, to whom others owe loyalty

LORD: a ruler or landowner with authority over a group of people

PAVILION: a small, temporary tent set up to hold a knight's weapons and armor during a tournament

PIKE: a short, heavy spear used by foot soldiers

SCABBARD: a sheath, or case, for a sword or knife

SENESCHAL: a person who manages the land and property of a lord

SQUIRE: a young person serving as a knight-in-training. Squires carried equipment, took care of horses, and performed other tasks for knights. In exchange, knights trained squires in combat and riding.

TOURNAMENT: a series of jousts or sporting battles fought at one time and place

WESTMINSTER: an area in south central England, part of modern-day London

WESTMINSTER ABBEY: a church and monastery, or religious house, at Westminster, England. The earliest monastery on the site dates back to the tenth century A.D. Westminster Abbey is the traditional site for all the coronations and burials of English kings and queens.

FURTHER READING AND WEBSITES

Crosley-Holland, Kevin. *The World of King Arthur and His Court: People, Places, Legend and Lore.* New York: Dutton Books, 2004. This illustrated guide provides information on key characters, daily life in a castle, knighthood, and other aspects of Arthurian legend.

King Arthur and the Knights of the Round Table
http://www.kingarthursknights.com
This website provides articles on the historical and legendary Arthur, a map and information on Arthurian sites, artwork, and the stories of the knights and other characters of the famous legend.

Roberts, Jeremy. *King Arthur.* Minneapolis: Lerner Publications Company, 2001. This book examines both the historical and the literary Arthur, showing how he became a legendary hero.

Steinbeck, John. The Acts of King Arthur and His Noble Knights. 1952. Reprint, New York: Farrar, Straus and Giroux, 1993. Novelist John Steinbeck retells Malory's Le Morte d'Arthur as a collection of tales.

CREATING *EXCALIBUR UNSHEATHED*

In creating the story, author Jeff Limke adapted *Le Morte d'Arthur*, written about 1485 by Sir Thomas Malory, an English knight. Artist Thomas Yeates used historical and traditional sources to shape the story's visual details—from the heraldic colors to the buildings of medieval London. Together the text and the art paint a portrait of the "once and future king"—the man who saved Britain and, legend has it, will return again when his country most needs him.

original pencil sketch from page 8

INDEX

ABOUT THE AUTHOR AND THE ARTIST

JEFF LIMKE was raised in North Dakota, where he first read, listened to, and marveled at stories of Arthur and his knights. Limke later taught these stories for many years and has written several adaptations of them. Some of his stories have been published by Caliber Comics, Arrow Comics, and Kenzer and Company. Right now, it's very safe to assume he's reading even more stories about Arthurian legend.

THOMAS YEATES Originally from Sacramento, California, Thomas Yeates began his art training in high school and continued it at Utah State University and at Sacramento State. Subsequently, he was a member of the first class at Joe Kubert's School, a trade program for aspiring comic book artists in New Jersey. Yeates is strongly influenced in his craft by old-guard illustrators like Hal Foster, N. C. Wyeth, and Wallace Wood. He has worked as an illustrator for DC, Marvel, Dark Horse, and many other companies, drawing Tarzan, Zorro, the Swamp Thing, Timespirits, Captain America, and Conan, among others. He has also edited *Al Williamson: Hidden Lands for Dark Horse.*